# A Bunch
# of Green
# Bananas

## DAVID GATWARD

First published in 1993 by
KEVIN MAYHEW LTD
Buxhall
Stowmarket
Suffolk IP14 3DJ

0 1 2 3 4 5 6 7 8 9

ISBN  0 86209 338 4
Catalogue No  1440303


Cover design by Jaquetta Sergeant
Typesetting by Louise Selfe
Printed and bound in Great Britain

# Contents

# Acknowledgements

Special thanks:

*Dad:* my editor and mentor, without whom this book would still be on 116 small bits of torn, coffee stained paper!!

*Gaynor, Geoff, Bryony, Hannah and Shona:* for being a family away from home.

*All at Marrick Priory:* for putting up with me, my mess and my appetite!

*Claire, Ken and Jackie:* your love, support and encouragement is something I will always remember.

*The 'Taizé' Bunch:* 'Laudate dominum!'

*Stan and Mary:* ('The Wrinklies') thanks for being so young at heart!

*Marcus Hazzard:* The Lord! A quality person with quite a smart, high quality hairstyle!

*Clair Rounding:* for being Yumski!

*Dave Wall:* (Fatty!) see you down Jackpot!

*John:* always remember, rubbing parsley on the knee cures rabbits on the ear – you nutter!

*Mr Kipling:* for your exceedingly good apple pies!

*This book is dedicated to my left hand,
which, although it had little to do
with the writing of this book,
supported me all the way!!*

# Foreword

Isn't fruit great? God's fantastic little snack that not only tastes good, but is healthy as well! Full of juicy goodness; sweet, delicious and laced with vitamins as a final touch! What a Master Chef! So, why bananas – green ones at that?

Well, if there's anyone who doesn't think a banana is funny then they need to have another look. Bananas are crazy! Not only do they taste good but they have a sense of the ridiculous that's unique! As Garfield, the cartoon cat puts it so well, 'They have entertainment value'. Who hasn't seen the comedy classic of someone slipping on a banana skin? God's amazing sense of humour wrapped up in something yellow, bent and edible. There seem to be no two bananas that are exactly the same. Small, large, bent, not-so-bent, ripe, unripe, bruised, and all hanging together on the same bunch.

And so it is with this book. Think of it as a bunch of bananas, with each prayer, poem, thought, whatever, different from that which precedes it and from whatever comes after it. You can pick from the 'bunch', and each 'banana' can be enjoyed for what it is, wherever you happen to find it. If the 'banana' seems ripe, savour it and enjoy all it has to offer, be it laughter, tears, thoughtfulness or anger. If you feel it needs time to ripen, leave it for a while and return to it later when you feel it's ready for your enjoyment. Just reach into the 'bunch' and enjoy the fruit!

# Ball rolling

Have you ever wished you hadn't started something because it was suddenly beginning to get out of control? Well, I have to admit that the thought has crossed my mind a few times since I began writing my first book, *Can We Talk, Lord?* The prayers it contained were very personal and were never originally intended for publication. They were for my own use, and expressed my feelings, my experiences and above all my struggles with the Christian faith and life in general.

When it was suggested that others might find them helpful, and that they should be put into print, I was catapulted onto Cloud Nine! Boy, was I happy, especially when what was happening dawned on me. People were actually buying the book, and finding that it was saying something that they were having a job to say themselves, but were desperately wanting to express. I received letters from people who not only enjoyed reading it but who found that God was speaking to them through it. People like Sandy who wrote:

> I felt I needed to write and let you know the encouragement I have received from your witness through the book.

I couldn't believe what was happening. 'Little ol' Dave' was having an effect on people and it was scary! Everyone enjoys the limelight but when I stood in it I wasn't so sure that it was where I wanted to be. Then it began to dawn on me that God was behind all of this, so what was I worrying about? He got me into it, and He'd take care of everything, and if the book was having any effect then it was

God's doing and not mine. If he could use what I was doing, then great! All I had to do was to trust him. That's still the case as I now put this book together. If God can use it, great – and if he does use it, and has used me, then what can he do with you and the things you can do for him?

Lord?
I'm scared.
Not a normal type of scared.
It's hard to explain, really.
This book thing was all exciting at the start.
I never really thought that it would have
    much impact.
I guess I was wrong.
You see, I thought I was in control.
I forgot you were.
And now?
Now I'm scared.
The book's selling, Lord.
Things are happening.
It's as though I started the ball rolling,
    and now I can't stop it.

So I'm faced with a choice:
    sink or swim.
Either I allow the ball to go out of control
    and crush me in its path,
      or I can do my best to keep up.

Easy choice I suppose.

I don't want to be crushed,
    but then I'm beginning to realise
    what it could mean
    if I allowed it to go on.
Do you realise where it could lead?
I could be asked to speak at things!
Do interviews!
People will know about me.
Expect me to be a certain way.
There's even an off-chance of 'fame!'
I know I wanted to be noticed, Lord,
    but don't you think this is going
    a bit too far?
I'm hardly personality material!
Just look at me!
I'm not special.
I'm as screwed up as the next person!
And my faith?
I forget to pray.
I don't read the Bible much.
I do the wrong things.
Open my mouth before my brain has a
    chance to stop it!
Why have you chosen me, Lord?
I've so little to offer.
I'm useless.
And scared.

'David, listen to me.
I chose you because I love you.
Have I ever put you into a situation
    we couldn't cope with together?
Remember, you always had a choice.
You could have said no.

You didn't.
Now take my hand and follow me.
You'll never face anything alone.
I'll always be there beside you.
Come, I'll show you the way.'

Amen.

# All I offered

This prayer gives me a very strange feeling as I read it again. I wrote it in the November of my 'A' Level year at Sixth Form College. It was a time in my life when I didn't really know what was happening to me. I'd messed up my mocks the year before and was therefore having to work twice as hard. I was in a local rock band and we had started doing a few gigs and were practising hard. And in the middle of all this there was me – confused, screwed up and depressed.

You only have to look at some of the prayers that I wrote at the time and that appear in *Can We Talk, Lord?* to realise the state I'd got myself into. Reading them now, I realise how I was often worrying unduly, and frequently getting over-anxious about things that ultimately don't matter very much. Yet at the time I really was confused and emotionally and spiritually depressed. And the reason? I'm still trying to figure that one out! One problem I can put my finger on was the loneliness I felt at the time. I wanted someone to confide in, a friend to talk to, share with, depend on. Knowing that, you can probably imagine how I felt when after giving a friend a birthday present they just handed it back to me and walked away.

That incident really brought home to me how much I needed friendship and yet also how vulnerable it makes us. I know it's only too easy to sit back and with a Colgate-bright 'Jesus loves me' smile to say 'I only need the Lord'. Now this may be true, but I believe there's more to it than that. I look at the Gospels and find that Jesus needed friends. He needed those he could talk to, confide in, have a good laugh with. He needed them, and yet as I read on and find myself in the Garden of Gethsemane with Jesus and those same friends, I find they let him down. They went to sleep, they ignored his pain, and he found that all he had left was his Father. And that's what I found – when all else fails he is still there, waiting open-armed to hold you close. Jesus knows how good it is to have friends, and also how it hurts when they let you down and leave you alone. So who better to talk to when that's where you are – left on your own?

Lord, don't you care?
So many times I've come to you for help,
    yet I hear no answer.
So many times I've needed comfort,
    yet there is none.
So many times I've put my trust in you,
    and wondered why.
Why me?
Why is it always me?
I know my problems are small compared to others;
    but to me?
To me they are heartbreaking.
It's so easy to say, 'Trust in Jesus!'
But how can I when it seems to make
    no difference?
What are you playing at?
Are you testing me?
Why, Lord?
What have I done?
Is there any purpose to it?
Whenever things start going right,

something happens, and I'm down again.
Down in the dirt.
Alone on my knees.
My fingers and hands cut and bleeding
    as I try desperately to pull myself up
    and start again.
But there is no rest.
No peace.

Do you know what it's like to have
    friendship thrown back in your face?
All I offered was a gift.
Nothing special.
Just something to bring a smile.

But it wasn't accepted.
A slap on the cheek.
It hurt, Lord.
Something so small,
    yet it hurt.
I could have cried.

But again, no one was there.

Lord?

Come to me, please.
I've kept on fighting.
But now?
Now I don't know.
It's as if I'm always alone.
Alone again.
To face things as one solitary heart.
Standing in the rain as the crowds rush by.

Not a glance, Lord.
Not one,
   caring,
   fleeting,
   glance.

'David, my son.
I know what it's like.
Believe me, I've been there.
All I needed was a helping hand.
The shoulder of a friend.
But they were asleep, David.
They were asleep.
I died for them, David.
I died for you.'

Amen.

# Being a friend

For some reason I seem to have a sponge-rubber shoulder! Anyway, that's how it seems, for I've had friends who've wanted to use it to soak up their tears. One friend calls me their psychologist, others treat me like an adopted brother. (Why do good looking girls say you're like a brother to them when that's not what you really had in mind?) I know this is what friendship is about and most of us do it for one another; it's one of the privileges of friendship. I know I often like to think that it's all down to my ability to listen, or to the charm of my amazing personality! But I've come to realise that I'm definitely fooling myself on both counts! What I do hope is that they see a little bit of Christ in me.

The idea that someone as confused as I am can be of help to others seems amusing, until you take account of God's place in things. I thank him that he can use me, that he's given me the sponge-rubber shoulder. We all need someone to talk to. Jesus may be the obvious answer, but so often he wants to provide the listening ear through someone else. He wants to use the shoulder they can provide, the arms that they can embrace with. To have a shoulder to cry on is a gift from heaven. To provide that shoulder is to help someone find something of heaven right next to them.

Lord, you there?
Can we talk?

17

You see, last night I helped someone:
A shoulder to cry on,
    a warm reassuring touch.
It's strange really.
But I seem good at it,
    know what to do,
    use the right words.
It makes me feel kind of special,
    the thought that I'm helping,
    healing,
    being a friend.
I can't explain it,
    the trust you feel as someone just lets go,
    releasing everything in a flood of tears,
    laying themselves bare.
    It's almost a privilege.

Sometimes I feel as if you're there too,
    helping,
    sitting with us, crying,
    sharing in that moment,
    comforting.
Like last night.
As she cried
    I knew you were there,
    holding her close.
Does it hurt you too, Lord,
    to see us upset?
Do you cry too?
Feel the pain?

'Yes, David, I feel it.
To see one of my children cry
    is one too many.

To see one upset,
   in pain,
   broken,
   it hurts.
Why?
Because I love you.
I love you all.
I love you so much
   I died for you.
I love you so much
   I gave up everything.
I love you so much
   that no matter how many times
   you turn your back on me,
   reject me,
   forget me,
   I still love you.
And last night, David,
   you felt that love.
Yes, I was there.
I sat with you and held you both,
   cried with you
   and comforted you both.
I'll always be there.
Just ask.'

Amen.

# Hey, good lookin'!

Every morning when I have to get up and look at myself in the mirror the thought that immediately enters my mind is a combination of 'Urgh!' and 'Help!' The reflection that stares at me through bleary eyes bears a distinct likeness to Cro Magnon Man – stubbled chin, knotted unkempt hair, dull unintelligent eyes.

It's all there. Even as I surface into something akin to consciousness it doesn't appear any better. Through eyes that are trying to get used to the idea of being awake and are showing a distinct lack of interest, I note that my chin has a marked similarity to a badly sown lawn, through which zits are doing their best to turn it into a scale model of a moonscape. A quick wash makes some difference, but it still doesn't stop me from believing that I look hideous.

Like most lads, I'd like to think that I was God's gift to the opposite sex – but that mirror daily reminds me that I'm not! And the closer I look at me, the less I like what I see. (Hey, that rhymes!) The trouble is, society emphasises the importance of appearance. Dress sense, a good physique, how you present yourself, your 'image', these are all so important. If you don't 'look right' you might as well give up! Fortunately God isn't so short-sighted – he's more interested in what we're like inside. I know that that can often be like glimpsing into the depths of a disgusting dustbin, but at least what's inside can be cleaned up and transformed by the power of his love.

With all our yukiness, grime and filth, he still loves us, and wants to change us. He sees what we are, and also what we can be. So, next time you look in the mirror and you see 'spot city' staring back – smile! God sees inside,

and he loves the person he sees and what that person can
become with his help!


Lord, why am I so ugly?
Every time I look in the mirror
    I want to hide away,
    or maybe even die!
Everyone seems so much more attractive
    than me!
I've worse acne for a start!
Now, there's a point, Lord;
    why did you create acne?
Is it a sadistic joke?
Something to tickle the
    ribs of the heavenly host?
Well, Lord,
    it's not funny!
I don't enjoy waking in the morning
    and looking at something
    resembling a pizza!
Nothing gets rid of them,
    not even surgical spirits!
(And believe me, I've tried!)
And then, Lord, there's the rest of me.
My ears are too big.
And my nose!
Now there's a subject for conversation.
Lord, they could use this
    to model a ski-jump on!
It's huge!
We've gone beyond Pinocchio,

and we're into elephant country here!
And what about the fact
    that my whole body seems to be
    strangely misshapen,
    perhaps even deformed!
Too thin, and yet too fat
    at the same time!
And my feet!
We're talking about battleships here
    and verging onto aircraft carriers!
Then finally,
    there's my hair.
Walk down the street
    and what do you see?
Nice hair,
    in good condition,
    stays in style . . .
Then there's mine!
I've come to the conclusion
    that my hair is alive,
    and none too pleased with
    the experience.
I look like a walking haystack!
'Oh, it can look great . . .
    for five minutes after combing.
Then it's a mess
    and even a blow dry doesn't tame it.
AAAAAARRRRRGGGHH!!!!

Lord, I'm sorry for being so ungrateful.
You created me,
    and in your eyes I'm beautiful
    (even if it's only you and my mum
    that thinks so!)

Help me to be satisfied.
I'm so lucky compared to some,
    yet I forget and get wrapped-up
    in having to 'look good'.

Help me to be more concerned about
    the 'inner me'.
And to stop hiding behind a false
    self-made 'image'.
Teach me, Lord,
    that it's not what's on the
    outside that counts,
    but that which is within,
    the image that is of the Creator.

Amen.

# Temptation

Temptation's strange – or that's the way it seems to me. I mean, what is it? We struggle with it every day of our lives. In my case that means a constant battle with laziness, gluttony, arrogance, and so on. But there are times when such temptations pale into insignificance, times when we feel a strong desire to deliberately and consciously go against God. And the thing is, those times seem to get more frequent. We don't know why we behave like this, we know we shouldn't, but we still do. Afterwards we feel so bad we swear that we'll never do it again. All I want to say is this, (well to be honest someone else said it, but I can't remember who!):

> 'Only when you want to go one way and God wants you to go another, and you choose God's way, will you truly know Jesus is your Saviour'.

Trust him and you won't go wrong. No matter how strange or how frightening it seems – always remember God loves you and will do nothing to harm you. He does know what is best.

Lord, it's about temptation.
Why do I always give in?
And why does it always seem strongest
    when I'm closest to you?
I don't *want* to give in to it . . .
    I just do.
And I don't know why.
I know it's Satan putting the boot in,

trying to mess up my life,
trying to turn me from you.
And Lord – sometimes I wonder if he's winning!
I begin to feel grotty inside,
   disgusting and unclean,
   not worth bothering about.
And then doubt sets in . . .
   'God doesn't exist . . .'
   'Life's pointless . . . '
   'I may as well give up . . . '
   'Blow everything' . . . '
But I can't.
The more I'm tempted,
   and the more times I give in,
   so I find,
   the more I come back to you.

The doubt can be overpowering,
   suffocating.
Yet somehow, there's a glimmer
   in the darkness,
   in your hand outstretched to me,
   in your love.
You keep me from falling too far,
   from giving in for good.
Lord, help me kick Satan from my life.
Let me show him he hasn't got a chance.
Help me to turn against temptation,
   and turn to you.
My friend.
My Lord.
My strength.

Amen.

# Where do I go?

Ever wonder where you're going – and why? When your life seems overcrowded with decisions, problems, responsibilities – and you just don't know what to do or where to turn. But then there are the times when God is definitely pushing you in a certain direction, and it's so clear and so definite and yet it all seems too crazy to be true. Just as it seemed for Jonah. Now, there was someone who really didn't want to do what God had in mind for him! Boy, did he do his best to hide from the Almighty! But what can be more crazy than trying to hide from God? You can't do it – he's everywhere and no matter where you may hide, he's still there knocking at your door!

Jonah eventually gave in – after nearly drowning and becoming a light snack for a passing fish! If God wants you to do something – then do it! There's no point hiding, you're wasting time, opportunity and life. Just do it!

Lord, where am I going?
I don't mean in a small everyday way,
    but more of a 'life-type' way.
What are your plans for me?
I seem to have had so many decisions
    to make lately.
Which A levels to take?
Do I take a year out?
What degree course should I do?
Which colleges do I apply for?

And after all that . . . ?
See what I mean, Lord?
It's so easy to get confused,
   lost in the muddle,
   to lose sight of you
   and of your will for me.
I know I should ask for your help in everything,
   every decision,
   every part of my life.
You should be there,
   helping me
   and sorting me out.
And yet I leave you out,
   I forget you,
   and usually do something stupid.
I'm sorry Lord.
I so want to do what's right,
   use my life,
   make something of it,
   have an impact,
   not disappear into obscurity,
   a life lived with no reason.
I want a reason,
   a purpose.
I want to live my life for you.

Help me, Lord.
Sometimes I get snowed under,
   bogged down with life
And I forget you're there.
Help me to get through life, Lord.
Please give me that purpose.
Show me where to go.
Guide me, Lord.

And when I get lost
   help me to find my way again –
   back to you.

Amen.

# Back home

I remember when I saw my family for the first time after leaving home. It was in Scotland (God's own country – regardless of what the Welsh, Irish or anyone else might say!) and I'd gone to join them for the weekend. I will never forget that train journey as I travelled through the breathtaking scenery, crossed the impressive desolation of Rannoch Moor and arrived in Fort William. I'll always remember getting off that train, rucksack thrown over my shoulder, clothes crumpled and untidy (that wasn't due to the journey – they're always like that), backside numb courtesy of British Rail. And there was my family, and I was home.

But how could I be home? I was then living in Yorkshire, and my family lived in sunny Humberside. But I was home because here were my roots. Throughout my childhood I've moved from one place to another, and as a result have no real allegiance to any place that I've lived. But Scotland is different, here are roots that go back through the generations; here there are relatives; here there is a family history; and whenever I head north there's that sense of going home – to the place of beauty, steeped in history, folklore and legend, and drawing me back to my origins and even my beliefs.

But I also felt I was home as I stepped onto that bleak railway platform because of those who were waiting there for me. Home cannot be contained in brick walls or defined by the boundaries of a small town. To come home is the experience of being with those I love and who I know love me.

And it's the same with God. To come home to God,

doesn't depend on where you are, but is an experience you can enjoy anywhere as you open yourself to his love. As my dad once said (he's so wise!) 'Imagine one hundred steps between you and God. He's taken ninety-nine of them and is there waiting for you to take that last one towards him'.

Take it – and wherever you are – you're home!


Jesus, can we talk?
I hope you don't mind.
I don't really know why I feel I must ask,
    because I know I don't have to.
You're my best mate.
Anyway, this may sound daft
    (or not – you are talking to me after all!)
But I don't know what to talk about,
    I just want to talk!
I guess that what's bothering me
    is you.
Not you as in *you*
    but the fact that so few *know* you.
And the fact that even though I can
    talk about it,
    write about it,
    and bore people to tears about it,
    I can't say I know you that well either.
I want to, Lord,
    I really do.
But I just keep failing.
Every downer,
    every pothole,

and I'm ready to quit,
give up,
run away.

But, for some reason,
    I keep coming back.

I sit and stew,
    fuming over what went wrong,
    crying over spilt milk.
Blaming everything,
    everyone,
    even you.

Yet . . .

I still come back.
I realise that what happened
    wasn't your fault
    but mine.
Not your mistake,
    but my stupidity.
So Lord,
    back home I come.
Back home
    to you.

Amen.

# Temper

Lord, can we talk?
I've got to talk to someone,
    and I know you'll listen.
It's about my temper.
It frightens me, disturbs me.
I can't control it.
One minute I'm fine.
Next – *pow*!

It's not that I lose my temper a lot,
    very rarely, in fact.
But when it happens,
    it happens in a spectacular way.
I know everyone gets angry
    (even you – remember that incident
    in the Temple?)
We can all strike out with words or fists,
    but then it's over, finished with.
But that's not what I mean.
One minute I'm fine,
    and then, one word out of place,
    or someone rubs me up the wrong way,
    and it begins to happen –
    my heart beats faster (so fast and strong
    that I can feel my chest heaving),
    the adrenalin starts pumping,
    my fists clench,
    I grasp things, squeezing them
    in frustration.
Then – it's as though tunnel vision takes over,

and I go quiet,
the calm before the storm.
All that fills my mind is anger,
fury,
wildness.
And it scares me.
I wish I wasn't like it.
I'm afraid that one day
it will really better me.
At the wrong time.
In the wrong place.
With the wrong people.

Lord, it frightens me.
Help me overcome it,
for I can't face it on my own.
It's like a wild animal trapped in a cage,
but the bars and the door are getting weak,
and one day they're going to give way.
Help me to stop that happening,
to tame the wildness,
to bring it under your care and your charge.
Lord please help me with my temper.
It's beginning to make me mad!

Amen.

# My image

Lord, is it cool to be a Christian?
It's just I was wondering, thinking,
    (actually being thoughtful for a change).
I don't know why.
I just found I was on my own,
    and was having a good look at my 'image'.

I suppose I've never followed the crowd.
I rejected the voice of the fashion conscious
    and listened to my own feelings and ideas.
I created an image for myself.
I believe you made us all to be special,
    unique.
And I've always enjoyed standing out,
    being different,
    being the way I wanted to be,
    believing what I believed to be true,
    and not just what others thought.

But now . . .

Now I see the image taking over.
It's smothering the real me, taking control.
And it's worrying.
I like being the way I am.
The long hair,
    the ear rings,
    the scruffy baggy clothes.
I like to appear happy-go-lucky, laid back.
It's not the hair that's the problem, however,

nor the clothes.
And it's not the music.
It's the attitude I'm adopting;
   that's what's bothering me.
It seems to take control.
It's like a defence mechanism,
   protecting my vulnerability,
   surrounding the weakness
   of my own self-esteem.
I want to be *me*,
   the person you created me to be.
But I'm too embarrassed,
   and so, there's the image.

Lord, please give me a hand.
I try to be like you.
And I keep on failing.
All mouth.
No action.
Letting the image take over.
Help me to stop trying to impress,
   to stop worrying about what others think.
And to only be concerned about
   what really counts –
   what *you* think.

Amen.

# Depressed

I can't remember when I wrote the next prayer, but as I read it again I'm sure it had something to do with a girlfriend. (That's hardly surprising as so many of my prayers seem to have their origins in one romantic disaster or another!) My track record with the opposite sex is hardly impressive – the longest relationship up to press (and here's hoping!) has lasted for the amazing length of seven weeks. Actually, the way that one ended illustrates my low placing in the Casanova stakes – I finished with her on her birthday of all days! I'm pleased to say we've grown a bit since then and are now the best of friends.

But what I'm getting at is, is there anything more painful or irritating than teenage love? One day you're in love – the next you're not. You plan for a date, and somehow your zits find out and decide to throw a party! It's a hard life! And then there are all the 'other' problems to deal with. It can't help but get you down. Now, of course, having matured into the wisdom of adulthood (who's fooling who?) I realise that so often I was making mountains out of molehills. And if back then I'd only tried to see things from God's side it would have all been so different – wouldn't it?

We all have a habit of listening to God when it suits us, and when it doesn't we go off on our own and do our own thing and as a result often end up hurt and let down. Why don't we realise that he's there because he wants to help and can help? Why do we forget that he's walked where we walk, felt what we feel – even teenage love!

Lord, I'm feeling really down.
And I don't even feel like speaking with you.
But – at least you'll listen to my moans.
It's rotten.
Life was looking really good
    for a while . . .
And now I'm depressed – again!
I sometimes wonder if I deliberately
    make myself depressed.
OK, I know something usually sets me off,
    but I encourage the process.
It's a sort of snowball effect;
    I just let it grow and grow
    until it's unbearable.
I forget that you're in control,
    and that all I have to do is trust.
But, it's easier said than done.
Why don't I listen to you?
'Let go and let God'
    is what I say so often,
    and then add,
    'There's nothing I'll come across today,
    that you and I can't handle together'.
I know it's all true,
    but then I back out of my side of the deal.
I do want to make the right decisions.
I don't want to hurt anyone
    (and that includes me!)
Lord, please help me,
    guide me,
    don't let me foul up again.
*Please.*

Amen.

# Lord, help my friend

One of the most painful experiences I've known so far (and I realise that I've hardly started the learning process that is life) is that of seeing a friend in trouble and being unable to do anything to help. The following prayer was inspired by just such an experience. All I had to do was sit there and watch a friend fall apart in front of me. To see someone you think a great deal of in tears, and yet to have no answers for them to grasp hold of is heartbreaking. Realising that there will be others who know just how I felt then, I'd love to be able to say I now know what to do, or what to say – but I don't, I'm still thinking and looking. All I can do is share something of that search and those thoughts with you, just as I shared it with the Lord in this prayer.

The words at the end of the prayer are an answer in themselves, for even as I prayed these words came. I don't feel they came from me at all – that's all I can say about them, but I hope they can help someone else as much as they helped me when they came.

> Lord, it's about my friend.
> A very special friend.
> She's in trouble,
>     messed up,
>     confused,
>     lost.
> Can you help her?
> Please, Lord.

I saw her just last week.
The first time in ages.
'Great', I thought.
Chat about old times.
Laugh.
Not so, Lord.
She was different.
Where there used to be a sparkle,
    there was nothing but a dark space.
Where there was an impish, friendly,
    fun-loving grin,
    now a look of sorrow.
I was lost.
There in front of me,
    a friend,
    a part of my life.
Cut.
Bleeding.
In need.
And I could do nothing!

Oh, how I wanted to reach out,
    just hold her close,
    comfort her.
But I couldn't.
There was a wall.
She needed help.
And I couldn't reach her.
Occasionally a brick would fall,
    some mortar would crumble.
But, once spotted,
    the small breach in the defences
    seemed to be filled
    with an even larger brick.

What do I do, Lord?
I want to help.
She needs something,
     someone.
She needs you.
How?
How do I get through?
Break down the wall?
I feel useless,
     unprepared.
But I want to help,
     dive into battle,
     fight for her.
And I need you to help.
Show me, Lord.
Guide me.

'David, listen to me.
Only you can show her my love.
I can't walk in until the door is opened
     from her side.
Show her the key.
Help her to do the opening.
She doesn't know how.
Yes, David, I can hear her,
     and I want to help.
But it's up to her.
Please bring her to me.'

Amen.

# Why?

Taizé is a Christian centre in France that thousands visit each year as part of their personal spiritual pilgrimages. Easter draws great numbers of such pilgrims from all parts of the world, and it's been my privilege to be amongst them. I must admit that after all the hype I'd received about it from others who had been there, I found the actual experience rather disappointing. There were aspects of that pilgrimage however, that were fantastic. I met so many different people, made some great (if short-lived) friendships, and found myself having to cope with a way of life and pattern of worship that was totally alien to me.

The food was a memorable shock. I have to admit to enjoying eating (some would call this an understatement!) and as a result, the Taizé breakfast menu of two pieces of French baguette and a blob of butter (unsalted!) plus a bowl of hot cocoa confused my gastronomic juices to say the least. The progression of meals through the day did little to relieve that confusion and disappointment. That was the food – then there were the services. Imagine sitting on a hard floor for an hour and a half (or more) three times a day. The expression 'numb bum' springs immediately to mind. If the physical discomfort could be overcome however, there was much that was helpful and memorable in these times of worship. There was the opportunity to sit, think and pray in a lovely, dark warm silence that has to be experienced to be believed.

It was in this sort of atmosphere that the following prayer was born. I was sitting there in the church, with other worshippers crowded around me, when suddenly the question hit me, 'Lord, why did you die?' After years of accepting the story and the circumstances of Jesus' death I began to realise that I wasn't so sure about what I did believe. So there in the service I quietly scrounged a bit of paper and a pen, and began to put my thoughts together. What emerged was this prayer, with the words tumbling over themselves as I wrote them down. This makes the prayer more special for me, as the words seem to bring me to the answer I'm looking for. Or more to the point, I believe that through the words God leads me to the answer I need. Isn't he great!

Lord, can we talk?
You see I'm feeling a bit lost.
It's 10 p.m. and I'm sat here with
    five thousand people,
    deep in prayer.
And I'm not.
I don't know why,
    I just can't seem to concentrate,
    focus my mind.
I've tried.
And failed.

I guess it's partly because I'm confused.
Through all these years
    I've accepted the fact of your death;
    not really thinking much about it.
Until now.
And, as I say,
    I'm a bit confused.
Why did you die, Lord?

It seems so pointless.
A lonely, painful death,
        for no apparent reason.
Why?
Surely there must have been another way?

And how come you died for me?
All those years ago?
I can't grasp it.
Make sense of it.
You died for me . . .
Why?
What for?
I just don't understand.

'David, listen to me.
I died because I love you,
        and everyone like you.
I showed the world the meaning of true love.
I was willing to die to save you.
Save you from yourself.
I forgave those who crucified me.
And even as the nails tore
        through my wrists
I still loved them.
I forgave them.

And I rose again,
        after all the pain,
        all the fear.
I rose again.
A sign of eternal hope.
A light in the darkness.
For you.

For everyone.
I died because I love you, David.
Love me . . .
Follow me.'

Amen.

# Dirty feet

One of the great things about God is that he loves us as we are. We can be the most grotty, disgusting individual, but God still manages to see us as we might become with his help. He sees the potential me, whilst loving the *actual* me!

There can't be many more irritating feelings than seeing someone tramp dirt through a house that you've just cleaned. In they march, and what was outside on the pavement now firmly sits on your best Axminster! Wonderful! So what do you do? You learn from the experience, you clean up and then make sure that no one else crosses the door step without first taking off their shoes. Compare that with God. Imagine him having a house. The front door is open in welcome. Someone strides in with muck all over their feet. They leave their dirt behind them wherever they go. God smiles and invites them into his front room! Of course, the dirty feet are a problem, so he asks the new friend how they came to be so dirty. As the story is told so he listens, and gently begins to clean those feet and wipe the dirt off the carpet.

When the friend steps outside again their feet are clean, unblemished. As they leave so someone else enters, only their face and their hands are as grimy as their feet. And God does the same for them only on a grander scale! Again and again this happens. Old and young, healthy and diseased, they all enter. Some have returned many times, their faces have become well known, the ever-dirty feet only too familiar. God doesn't complain. He just helps us clean up and sends us on our way with renewed confidence and determination to stay that way. He loves us – dirty feet and all!

Lord. Hi!
About five minutes ago something
    strange happened.
My brother walked into my bedroom.
Strange? No, not usually.
That is, it wouldn't have been
    if he hadn't been carrying an engine
    from a 125 cc motorbike in his arms!
It brought a smile to my face
    to say the least!
There he was,
    muck and grime all over his shirt.
In his arms – an engine.
And on his face?
The proudest grin I've ever seen.
There it shone for all the world to see.
As if saying, 'Look, Dave! I did it!
I got it off! Great, eh?'
And it was at that moment it hit me.
What it is to be in a family, all together.
I was writing but he wanted to show me
    what he'd achieved.

Mum and dad were painting
    the bathroom (how romantic!)
But they also had to share the moment.
You see, Lord
    we take an interest in each other.
If one does something they're chuffed about,
    then they tell the rest.
Share the happiness.
Even if it does mean carting
    a greasy engine upstairs
    into a freshly painted room!

There are so many homes
    where you have to take your shoes off
    before you go in.
It's to avoid getting the carpet dirty.
'Yes, you can come in
    as long as you don't make a mess.'

OK, I'll agree,
    they're lovely houses.
But they don't feel like homes.
They can be cold,
    clinically clean.

Our house?
Well, we charge in, shoes on, coats soaked,
    and we just plonk down in front of the fire!
Of course we clean our shoes,
    but that's not the point.
The point is that we can come in as we are.
We don't have to discard our rubbish
    at the door.
It comes in with us.

A bit like your family, Lord.
You accept us as we are.
Disgusting and grotty.
No sign commanding us to clean our feet
    before entering.

Thank you for that, Lord.
For accepting me.
Dirty feet and all.

Amen.

# 'The one and only'

Most of us wonder what it would be like to be wealthy, although some don't have to wonder – they know! For the rest of us however, the long tree lined drive graced by the country mansion with the Porsche parked outside – is all a dream. I really do wonder, though, if such a lifestyle is all it's cracked up to be. (It would be great to get the opportunity to find out, just to quench my thirsty curiosity – and boy would I enjoy it!) It's all wishful thinking, and quite honestly I don't know if more possessions would make me any happier.

When I reach some great age and start to look back, I can't see me being over concerned about the car I had in 1992, or the stereo I bought at that time. It's more likely that I'll remember the people I met, the friends I made, the love and happiness I enjoyed, and such matters as the size of my income or the number of rooms I occupied are all going to seem insignificant. It makes me realise that I should spend less time worrying about how much I want, and appreciate all that I already have. To think of reaching the end of my life and feeling that I've never really lived it, disturbs and worries me.

Life is God's precious gift to us, and the way we live it is our way of saying thanks. It's up to us to make it the biggest, most wonderful expression of gratitude that we can!

Lord, do you listen to music?
I suppose that's a daft question,
    when I think of all the music
    that erupts from your churches!

If you don't listen to it,
    and if you don't enjoy it,
There's an awful lot of people
    who've got you weighed up wrong!
Anyway, there was this song.
It was called, 'The one and only'.
Actually it wasn't bad,
    quite catchy,
    good beat.
But it's not the numbers chart potential
    that concerns me,
    but that title, 'The one and only'.
You see,
    it seems to me, Lord,
    that there's an epidemic just now,
    brought on by some sort of
    mind-melting bug.
And it's getting out of control.
(I know I'm probably doing it again –
    getting over-dramatic –
    but this is bothering me.)
What's happening
    (the symptoms of the epidemic)
    is that people (and I include myself)
    only seem to be bothered
    about themselves.
Looking after 'Number One'.
And it's scary, Lord.
You ask folk why they do the job they do,
    and though a few say, 'Because I enjoy it',
    or 'Because I feel it's right for me',
    so many others will answer,
    'It's just for the money'.
Hours endured.

Weeks and months put up with.
And so often talents, abilities, potential –
    all wasted.

I know I'm as bad as anyone else.
I plan my career around the size
    of the prospective wage-packet.
I want money.
I need money.
Especially now, Lord.
I suppose there's no point in asking you
    if you know how to get by
    on a student's grant?

The problem is – getting things
    into perspective.
Money is necessary.
Food.
Clothing.
Education.
Leisure.
All have a price tag to them.
And no sooner have I cash in my pocket,
    than it seems to be gone.
There's one problem, Lord.
Sorting out a realistic budget to live on,
    and then another's keeping it!
But the real problem is this
    over-concern with wealth.
This concentration on personal
    wants and desires,
    above everything else.
Lord, help me sort it out,
    for I can't think of a solution.

I need money for my college,
    my work,
    my life in general.
But I'm afraid I'm getting (have got?)
    greedy.
Help me to get by.
To realise what really matters –
    that the 'one and only'
    who really counts,
        isn't me.
But you.

Amen.

# You let me be me!

Do you like yourself? It might seem a strange question, but I don't think it is. For I can't see what's wrong with liking who and what you are. Now, I'm not talking about being bigheaded, informing the world that 'I like myself because I really am rather wonderful'. I'm talking about liking yourself for what you are. In fact I believe it's something Jesus encouraged us to do – to have a sense of self-worth, personal dignity.

Remember how he said that the most important commandments are that you should 'love the Lord your God with all your heart, soul, mind and strength', and 'your neighbour as much as yourself'. So it could be that if you have a low opinion of yourself, and don't like who you are, you're going to find it difficult to do as Jesus asks. If you don't think much of yourself, maybe you'll find it hard to think much of your neighbour! Anyway, if you don't like yourself, what are you saying about God – that he doesn't know what he's doing? He thinks you're great! He loves you so much that his Son died for you – has he got it all wrong? Go on – try loving yourself – God loves you!


Lord, I've got this really great poster.
There's this cute little porcupine,
    with its eyes looking out at you.
And above it the words simply read,
    'Thank you dear Jesus,
    for letting me be me.'
Brilliant and true!

You let us,
    be us!
It's so straightforward,
    but so good to know!
We don't have to change to be
    someone else.
You want us to be the person we are.
The one you created us to be.
And you want us to enjoy the experience!

I love being me!
(No one else would want the job anyway!)
And to have your permission!

You love us as we are,
    with our strangeness,
    our quirks,
    our moods,
    everything.
Our entire humanness.
And you love us for it.
Every individual.
You see the good, and the potential in us all.

We may be pretty poor examples
    of what you intended.
And yet, it doesn't change
    how you feel about us.
In all the immensity and power
    of your greatness,
    you love each single,
    unique person.

Of course, I could ask, 'Why?'

But I don't need to.
You love us, because . . .
You love us.
There is no other answer.
It's the way you are.

Thanks Lord,
    for just making me me!

Amen.

# Homework

Homework – how I loved it! How I miss it, and now yearn for those nights spent in serious concentrated study! Well, if you believe that you'll believe anything. I hated it and I now hate the memories of it. Evenings of biology and English, history and maths, and the ever-present problem of getting down to some real work. Although, looking back, I realise that I'd become a craftsman in the art of 'putting things off'.

An announcement that I was starting my work at 7.00 p.m. forestalled any parental hassles between end of school and 7.00 p.m. As the clock struck seven, I'd enter my room and start the preparations (so important). Books to unpack, pencils to sharpen, implements (the fancy name for well-chewed pens and broken-ended rulers!) to arrange, and so on. This could be spun out until 7.45 p.m., when I could justify my plea that it was time for a coffee. A coffee had to include other refreshments to keep up my flagging strength, and so at least fifteen minutes would be needed to raid the fridge, make sandwiches and so on. Then back to the next task – the compiling of the evening's homework diary. 'Sir said we must do it' – so we do it, and take another hour or so to plan out what we should really be doing! So the evening is spent and I descend the stairs with ruffled hair and weary look, suggesting that I am as well!

It's easy now to laugh at it, but the problem is that old habits die hard and I still find it difficult to get down to things. My mind has a tendency to wander all over the place and it struggles with my attempts at a disciplined timetable or work programme. But at least I do now try to achieve both of these. I try to set myself goals, things I intend to achieve, and I then go for them with as much energy and enthusiasm as I can find. If the distractions come, and the mind wanders, then I try to talk it through with God, and get things sorted out and my mind clear so that I can get down to my work.

I try to adopt the same sort of approach to my faith, for that too can just drift aimlessly. I find it a problem putting my mind and effort into being a Christian. It seems so hard, so difficult. Then I remember the business of having a goal, and I look at the ones Jesus opens up for me. Everlasting life, forgiveness, peace, eternal undying love – and that's just the start! I set my mind on the job in hand and go for it! And it's worked.

I know the picture I've just painted will be familiar to many. Maybe the way God's helped me sort it out will be of help to someone else as well.


Lord, I can't think.
I've been sitting here for ages,
    and my mind hasn't moved any further
    than my backside.
It's ground to a halt.
As I try to concentrate on something,
    anything,
    it just seems to go blank.
Take now for example.
I want to talk with you,
    my God, my Creator,
But my mind refuses to get into gear.
It just idles in mental neutrality.
And so no matter how I rev it,

it goes nowhere!
I can't think of the words I want to say.
My mind seems an empty maze,
    of mixed-up nothingness.
And I'm lost somewhere in the middle.
I hate this when it happens,
    because it happens so often,
    on so many occasions.
And usually at the worst possible time.
How many times when I've got jobs to do,
    deadlines to meet,
    does my mind switch off,
    or adopt a deliberate 'go slow' policy?

Lord, help me sort out this mess in my head.
To get my mind and thoughts under control.
And help me to realise that even though
    it often seems the job will never get done,
    if I put my mind to it,
    really knuckle down,
    and at the same time, look to you for help,
    then it will!
Help me to realise that
    such miracles can happen!

Amen.

# Raining

Lord, it's raining again.
And once more I'm stuck indoors.
With nothing to do.
I suppose I could write a book,
    paint a masterpiece,
    compose a symphony:
But somehow,
    I don't think so.
So, how about a chat?
Can I ask,
    'Do you bother about the weather?'
Because we Brits revel in it.
It's our main topic of conversation,
    guaranteed to grab anyone's
    immediate interest.
I suppose it's all because it's
    so unpredictable,
    so variable.
It can be windy,
    wet,
    cold,
    and possibly,
    if you're quick enough to notice,
    even sunny.
So many mornings we wake up,
    stretch,
    open the curtains,
    and prepare ourselves for another
    swim to work!
But when the sun does make an appearance . . .

*wow!*
Then we're talking major excitement!
Allow the temperature to hover above
    10 degrees,
      and everyone's into shorts,
      having barbecues,
      and piling off to the beach.
Me included!
Anything for that tan!
Which, of course,
    turns to rust the next day
    when it rains!

In a way, it's a bit like life,
    this weather.
Mentally,
    emotionally,
    spiritually,
    it can seem as if it's always raining.
Depression,
    confusion,
    sadness,
    'Can't be botheredness',
    all pour down,
    and soak and freeze us
    in our personal misery and self-pity.
But occasionally a break comes in the clouds,
    and the sunshine of
    happiness,
    laughter,
    joy,
    love,
    beams upon us.
And life's great again.

Lord, it's these moments of
    inner warmth and light,
    that help us cope with the days
    that are grey,
    and the nights that are starless.
You never promised that life would be easy.
You never deceived us into imagining
    that Christianity made 'heaven on earth'
    a guaranteed certainty.
What you promised,
    and prepared us for,
    is what we now have.
As one poet put it,
    'Strength for the day,
    Rest for the labourer,
    Light for the way,
    Grace from the trial,
    Help from above,
    Unfailing sympathy,
    And undying love.'

Amen.

# Group fellowship

The following two pieces have a similar theme, and both are concerned with thoughts I've had running round in my mind about the church and all its different 'bits'. The first was written whilst I was at a church-based conference when I found myself asking 'Where on earth do I fit into all this?' As I'm sure that most other folks in the churches find they're often asking the same thing, I include it now in the hope that something in it will be of help to others who get as confused with the churches as I do.

The second is a more humorous (I hope!) look at the churches. Believe me, that's the way it's intended and I hope no one is hurt by it! I really do believe that if we'd only step back a bit and try to see things from God's perspective, no matter how muddled or confused they may seem at first, they will eventually seem much clearer. I also believe that when you look at things from God's angle, the humour and comedy that's there in so much of life begins to come through. So hopefully, God will help you enjoy what follows and get you laughing – not just at others, but at yourself!

Lord, You got a minute?
It's just that I'm at a bit of a loose end –
   sitting here wondering,
   as folk all around me are busy talking,
   and getting involved in 'deep discussion',
   'Heavy fellowship'.

And a thought crosses my mind.
Why do we all seem so different?
Why do I get on better with some,
    than others?
How is it
    we all do things so differently?
You know how I've never found
    this 'group fellowship' stuff easy.
The 'opportunity' for open prayer
    has always felt uncomfortable –
    especially when I've been expected
    to say something!
What do I say?
What do they expect me to say?
And Lord, why does it make me so nervous?
Me,
'Bubbly Dave',
'Mr Loud'.
The Extrovert with a capital 'E'.
Nervous.
Tongue-tied.
Embarrassed!
I can't make it out, Lord.

And another thing.
When I do get involved,
    I feel everyone else is better at it than me.
Their words flow.
Their prayers make sense.
They seem so fluent.
What am I doing wrong?
Am I inferior?
Do I worship the wrong way?
Is there something wrong with my faith?

What I reckon, Lord,
     is that there's a bit of you in all of this.
Everyone's an individual.
Created as a unique masterpiece,
     by you, the Master Craftsman.
And in this individuality I see
     the variety that you love so much.
We're all different.
Do things differently.
Express ourselves (and our prayers)
     in different ways.
It's no wonder we end up with friction
     in the Church,
     and between the churches, Lord.
But we share one thing in common,
     that overcomes all the differences,
And that's you,
     and the love you have for us.
Thanks, Lord!

Amen.

# The Church – a guided tour

Our church it is a strange little place,
A place where you can go
And sit and praise your Lord on high,
Or complain about him below!

Churches here and churches there,
Small ones, big ones too,
But the question is which one to choose?
The one God calls you to.

Of course, we know they're all 'just fine',
At least that's what they say,
But upon entering some, a thought seems to come,
'Why on earth did you choose to stay?'

Let's take for a start the Methodists,
A stern and hardy breed.
To keep alive the fire inside,
A 'hymn sandwich' is all they need!

Committee meetings, Sunday School,
Coffee mornings galore,
And carefully placed collection plates,
Put at every door.

That's not your scene? You don't feel sure?
Don't worry, no please don't fret.
There's plenty more for you to try,
To please your Christian palate.

Perhaps you're more the serious type,
Who likes to sit and pray,
Then try the Church of England
And maybe there you'll want to stay!

Of course, at first it may seem strange
On your very first Sunday,
As you begin to wonder if you should
Stand up, sit down, or pray!

'Which board is for which book?' you ask,
And why is it so cold?
And what about the warbling choir?
They look so bloomin' old!

'More life!' I hear you scream at last!
Some songs and choruses too!
Just follow me and we'll go next door
I've just the place for you.

'Jesus loves you!' It says outside
In letters big and bold.
It's just for those who didn't know –
And thought you should be told.

So in you go, you never know,
It might be just OK,
The songs they sound quite cheerful,
And the band can actually play!

There's people dancing in the aisle
Their hands up in the air.
And you feel your foot start tapping
Just as the pastor calls for prayer.

Suddenly they're at it again!
Their hands up to the sky!
And behind you a voice says something like,
'Acomb kanaski nobye'!

'What are they saying?' you have to ask,
But you're straightaway interrupted,
As someone from the front calls for
'A testimony from Brother Richard!'

Now this goes on, and on, and on,
Then some choruses ('just one or two more!')
So although you came in at 10.45,
You don't leave till half past four!

Back home you sit and wonder what
You really have to do,
And with hands clasped together you ask the Lord,
What he reckons is best for you.

You think about the different prayers
And songs and choruses too,
And how it is they're all so keen
About their message getting through.

Then a voice inside, just chuckles and says,
'You do what's best for thee!
As for myself I enjoys it all,
For I love such variety'!

# 'Nothingness'

Doing nothing, chillin' out, slobbing out, what ever you want to call it – everyone does it (or is that 'doesn't'?) So – what's wrong with it? In our wonderfully organised materialistic world it's easy to feel guilty about doing nothing. You work all day, spend the evening in the gym, or playing squash, and then prepare for a hectic weekend of football, golf, gardening, whatever. The point is you don't just stop, and do nothing. It goes right back to childhood, when your parents insist that you 'Don't just sit there, do something!' We must 'do'.

Now I'm not saying we should be lazy (I personally don't need any encouragement on that score), and the last thing we need is a world of people just sitting back and wasting life. What I do believe though, is that every so often we all need to take time out from the world, sit back and let go for a while. It's the way we can often get life back into perspective. The Bible says that God created the world in six days, and on the seventh? He rested. So, next time you feel you 'want out' for a while, why not just hang up a sign on you door, 'Doing nothing – Boss's orders!'

> Lord, I hope you don't mind,
>     but today I did
>     NOTHING!
> And Lord, I'm proud of it!
> It makes a change.
> So often I seem to be running round

like someone possessed.
Trying to get things done.
Rushing from one job to another.
So, today I thought,
    'Blow it,
    I'm going to be lazy.'
I got up
    (after long negotiations with my bed,
    which seemed determined
    not to release me).
 Then there was breakfast,
    quickly followed by dinner
    (somehow they seemed to overlap).
And then – bath time.
You can't beat an hour or two,
    luxuriating in hot water,
    with the humour of a pile
    of 'Asterix' books,
    loudly accompanied by Radio One.
Bliss!
Eventually,
    I washed,
    lolloped out.
Got dressed.
And eased my way downstairs.
Put on a video,
    and watched a film until tea time.
Now, Lord, I'm in bed.
I've had tea,
    and supper.
And now I stretch out between clean sheets
    with every muscle totally relaxed.
I guess I should feel bad
    I've 'wasted' a day.

I could have got something done.
'Achieved something worthwhile'.
But Lord,
    I thank you for this one small
    oasis of nothingness.
Today I was lazy.
And I thank you for it!

Amen.

# My mouth

There's nothing more embarrassing than opening your mouth and putting a pair of size elevens straight into it! And I should know – it happens frequently! I hate upsetting people and I especially don't like falling out with friends. But I seem to be very skilled at arranging the former and achieving the latter. My problem is that unlike those folk who can hide their feelings, I can't – my emotions, views, beliefs are bared for all to see. I often wish I could keep quiet, or at least engage my mind before I put my mouth into gear, but the more I try, the more I'm forced to realise that that's not me. I am what I am and God still loves despite it!

You just have to look at Simon Peter, to see what I'm getting at. He was one of those who were closest to Jesus, and yet he seemed to have just this problem. Hot-headed, he tended to speak first and think later. But look at how God used him. In this I see hope for myself – and all others like me. God can use anyone, no matter what sort of person they are. He *can* use you, even if your mouth *is* as troublesome as mine!


Lord, it's about my mouth.
Why?
Why have I got it?
OK, there are the obvious answers,
    like eating.
Like it?

I love it!
My mouth gets full use there!
Breathing.
In, out,
    taking in the oxygen,
    releasing carbon-dioxide.
I not only do it,
    but I understand what I'm doing.
It's not these things that bother me, Lord,
    but the fact that I seem to have been born
    with a mouth that has a mind of its own!
A spirit that is independent
    of any other part of me.
Just get me annoyed,
    slightly angry,
    or just plain miffed,
    and before I know what's happening,
    my mouth's into overdrive,
    before my mind's even engaged first gear!
Every time I dread it happening again,
    but it's too late,
I've opened my mouth,
    and firmly filled it with
    a pair of size eleven boots.
Of course I could stop,
    say 'Sorry'.
But no, not me,
    not now.
'I'm going to have my say.
Give my victim their money's worth!'
And so I embarrass them,
    upset them,
    hurt them.
And afterwards,

all I can do is question 'Why?'
As I feel the shame and hurt deep inside.

O Lord, I know that some might think it funny.
But for me it really is a serious matter.
I say so many things I don't mean.
I cause pain when it's the last thing
    I want to do.
And I keep on doing it.
Help me control it, Lord.
Help me to shut my mouth,
    for I know how I must irritate others.
Because I'm even getting on my own nerves!

Amen.

# When the going gets tough

Lord, I want a chat.
You see, it's about life.
Mine specifically.
But also life in general.
It's recently dawned on me
    that living isn't very easy,
And being a Christian doesn't always
    make it any easier!
I know it's not a world shattering revelation –
    in fact I can't think why all my
    bouts of depression,
    morbid feelings,
    and generally miserable outlook,
    haven't brought me to this realisation before.
But there it is –
    I now realise how life can be as
    difficult for me
    as for anyone else.
I'm not being defeatist (honest).
But it's just that I always seem to be
    faced with decisions
    about what's right and wrong,
    about what I should do, or not do,
    about morality – and what that
    means for me.
Then in addition – you expect us to be
    charitable,
    thoughtful,
    kind,
    caring.
We're not supposed to be

angry,
proud,
boastful.
(And Lord when I've done something
I'm proud of.
I want to boast about it –
does that mean I've got it wrong
on both counts?)
You don't like us getting
awkward,
greedy,
rude,
foul mouthed.
And the list goes on.

To be truthful, Lord,
I have to admit to liking the do's
and not being over-keen on
the don'ts.
I want to be charitable and generous,
and I don't want to be awkward
and greedy.
I don't like being a first class ratbag.
But that's the trouble.
I find it hard not to be.
It's tough doing what's right,
and avoiding those things that are wrong.
And when the going does get tough,
I've a tendency to retreat,
to back off,
to go home and make a cup of cocoa!

I'm sorry, Lord.
I look at my pathetic attempts to be

what you want,
and I realise how disappointed
you must be in me.
But I do want to keep trying.
I don't want to give up.
And when the going does get tough,
Lord, help me to remember
you're there with me.
Just to keep me going!

Amen.

# No chance!

What are we here for? What a question! It's baffled and occupied some of the greatest minds since the dawn of time, and so I'm not going to add to the masterpieces of literature and philosophy with a rundown of my own pet theories. Wouldn't it be great though, if when we were born there could be a little note pinned on us by the Creator, saying 'This one is here to be a writer', or it could be musician, mechanic, nurse, accountant, brickie, whatever. It would solve a lot of problems, knowing what we are actually here for, what we've got to do, and which direction in life we need to take.

Unfortunately, it's not that easy, but then, God never intended life to be as dull and uninteresting as that would make it! Instead he gives us guides – indicators to follow and to use to get our bearings. Through prayer, reading the Bible, listening to people we trust and so on, the way ahead can start becoming clear. We might make a wrong turn here and there, but I can't believe that God has only one possible plan for our lives and that if we get it wrong we've then fouled things up for good. It doesn't work like that.

When we do go wrong, providing we recognise it and ask for his help, he sorts us out, brushes us down, makes sure any cuts and bruises are dealt with, and then he sets us back on the path. Because of what we've done, or failed to do, the path may now take a different turn, but he's adapted his purposes and given us a new plan to follow. The important thing is to trust him, and to follow him. The way ahead may never seem easy or even appealing, but he'll never allow it to test us beyond our capabilities, and we can always guarantee it will be

stimulating, challenging and fulfilling. Believing that –
who wants it to be easy?


Lord, I hope you don't mind me asking, but . . .
Has anything of any use come from me?
Look at me. I'm a waste of space, really.
Mixed-up ideas. Crazy views.
As screwed-up, weird,
    and strange as you'll ever get.
So, what use am I?
I know you've got a really good
    sense of humour, Lord,
        but I'm beginning to feel I'm the one
        who doesn't get the joke
        when everyone around me is laughing!
What is my purpose?
My reason for being here?
I wish you'd tell me.
I'm really wanting to believe in you,
    trust you.
But right now I just can't see where
    it's getting me.
Can't you give me a hint
    as to the direction I need to take?
Somewhere it says that you're the potter
    and we're the clay.
So how about it, Lord?
I'm tired of being the sticky lump
    on the potter's wheel.
I want to move on.
Become what you want me to be.

So that when I look
  and wonder if anything good
  will come from me,
  you'll be able to show me
  that it already has.

Amen.

# Dear Boss

I enjoy birthdays, and I get a kick out of Christmas – because I love getting presents. I'm a living example of the Garfield cartoon – always ready to let others know when the big days are and how I'd be most appreciative of their kindness, etc, etc!

It was the same when I was younger; the only difference was that then I didn't appreciate the importance of the 'Thank you' letters'. I dreaded having to write them, and could always find excuses for putting off the moment when well-chewed biro was applied to dog-eared paper. (A bit like writing this book really!)

Now, though, I realise how good it is to say thank you. It not only shows you appreciate the gift, but actually helps you think about the giver, their kindness, thoughtfulness and so on. It makes you realise how much they do think of you. So here goes with a 'Thank you' letter to the most generous giver of all.

Dear Boss,
Over the last few years as we've become friends and grown closer together, I've come to realise how important you are to me. You've always been there when I've needed a helping hand. Be the problem large or small, it's made no difference – you've always turned up to offer help.

You've picked me up, and brushed me down so many times when I've fallen. When I've got into situations I couldn't handle, you've soon arrived to help me sort things out. When I've been hurt and only able to cry and let the pain pour out, you've been there with the sympathetic shoulder I needed. In the darkness you've come and, taking my hand, led me back into the light of day. And always, you've asked nothing in return.

And do you remember the times when we laughed together? Sitting there, smiling, joking, happiness in our eyes as the tears rolled down our cheeks?

Yet still, amongst all of this, there were times when I turned away, ignored you, even passed you in the street without acknowledging your presence. Even when you were hurt, hungry, helpless – as you so often are in the needy who are your children – I still turned away. I left you there, and often didn't even think about what I was doing.

That's what hurts the most, especially as it made no difference to you. You just kept on loving me, and when I came back, you received me with open arms. You loved me with an undying love. You have loved me, and have demanded nothing, expected nothing in return. Always there, always waiting to help, and all I can say is 'Thank you'. Thank you, my friend, for being my Friend.

Yours always,

David

# Driving test

Lord! I've passed my driving test!
Boy – am I pleased!
Free at last!
On the road.
Wow! What a buzz!
I can't believe it –
    the test was easy!
(OK – I know I failed last time!)
But it was fantastic.
Those words,
    'I'm pleased to tell you you've passed'.
I had to phone home straight away,
    tell them the good news.
(If it is good news to any parent
    that their offspring can now be unleashed
    onto the public highway!)
But I'm so pleased.
It's as if I've taken the next great step
    into adulthood.
I'm that bit closer to independence,
    being self-reliant.

Help me Lord,
    to make use of it.
Help me to at least try and be sensible,
    and not just be another 'boy racer'.
Help me to drive carefully.
And thoughtfully.
Sensitively.
And most of all – safely!

And Lord,
    please help me to remember
    what to do at a box junction!

Amen.

# Silently screaming

Lord, why is the news always so depressing?
Whenever I switch on the TV
    all I see is pain,
    suffering.
Thousands of pairs of eyes
    staring out at a world
    they cannot see,
    and will never know.
Silently screaming.
Begging for help.


And I sit there,
    feeling useless,
    inadequate,
    as those eyes of pain
    silently screaming, fade into oblivion.


Lord, what am I to do?
I want to reach out and help –
And yet I keep my hands firmly clenched
    in my pockets,
    tight grip on my money.
I want to learn why it happens,
    what causes such pain.
But I switch off,
    unwilling to be disturbed out of my apathy
    and self-interest.
And so I continue with my life.
Wander through the hours and days

that are filled with material pleasures:
food,
drink,
comfort
warmth,
music,
video.
Until in the evening I'm again
watching the News,
viewing the same scenes,
being confronted by those same faces.
Their eyes still searching,
silently screaming,
as in the eye of the camera
another child dies
in the arms of its dying mother,
and another food convoy fails to get through.

It continues,
and continues,
as we in the West
ignore their pleas,
too busy with the 'more important matters'
such as presidential elections,
the money market,
stocks and shares,
the weather.

And democracy
democratically decides to ignore the problem,
turn its back.

There are no votes in it.
Why give money which can be spent here?

And so they keep on dying,
    and the desert is allowed to glut itself
    on their pain.
Barren of life, void of water.
Fed only by ignorance and apathy.

Lord, help me!
I honestly don't know what to do!
Faced by this problem,
    I remember Moses.
The way you showed him how a starving people,
    lost in a desert, could still be fed.
And so, Lord, I pray
    that you will show us
    in the wilderness of our making,
    how we might feed the silently screaming,
    starving children of today.

Amen.

# And the world

Lord, I'm frightened.
For me.
For the world.
For the human race.

In all our greatness,
    all our diversity,
    we don't seem wise enough
    to understand what we're doing
    to our earth –
    and to ourselves.

Thirsty for power,
    hungry for wealth,
    we feed off your creation,
    our appetite unsatisfied,
    our greed unquenched.
Until the food runs out.
And the world runs down.

Oil,
    coal,
    metals,
    wood,
    water,
    plant life.
Resources so finite,
    so necessary for our survival,
    irrationally used,

irresponsibly wasted,
until lost forever.


Rain forests disappear.
Species of plant
     and animal vanish,
     never to be seen again.
And the world looks on
     with gathering dismay
     at the ineffectiveness of its campaigns,
     and the indifference of bureaucracy.
And so we scream
     and shout in our frustration.
We bang against the unmoving doors
     of government and vested interest,
     in the hope and prayer
     that someone will stop the insanity,
     and bring an end to the sacrilege.
For, Lord,
     this is your world,
     your Creation,
     your masterpiece.
A paradise in the cosmos.
A place of incredible,
     divinely inspired beauty.
Alight with the life that you first gave.


Please, Lord,
     help us.
Help us, we who are too often blind
     to our own stupidity,
     lost in our own greed,
     and dying because of our indifference.

Heal our eyes that we may see.
Bring us back to where we should be.
Halt our dying, that we may live again.
Make us whole,
   so that your world may be healed.

Amen.

# These city streets

Lord, sit by me,
   for I feel suffocated by the problems
   of the world,
   that find their way onto
   our own city streets.
As I gaze out and gasp in horror
   at the plight of the victims
   of war,
   famine,
   oppression –
   so my eyes are too easily closed
   to the victims closer to me.
The homeless.
The addict.
The single parent.
All, who are so easily sucked
   into the whirlpool of despair
   and loneliness.

In our world of people
   it's ironic that, as the population
   expands,
   so loneliness appears to grow.
People die through being alone,
   whilst the rest of us
   try to ignore the problem,
   cover it up,
   put it at the bottom of the pile.

But the pile gets bigger,
   as we continue to add to the bottom,

pushing individuals and families into that
struggling,
suffering,
lower strata of our society.
Until we are faced with
a mass of such loneliness
that it touches even us.
We try to escape,
and in desperation reach out,
for anything,
anyone,
to relieve the sense of being alone.
We run and run,
only to find that others have tried,
and become tired,
until, exhausted, they litter our streets
with their cardboard box homes,
no longer alive to live,
but merely to exist,
continue,
survive.

As the numbers keep growing,
as more and more are swept into
the never-ending pile
by the unthinking bulldozer
of bureaucracy;
as they fade into obscurity,
losing sense of beginning and end,
lost in the insidious, creeping jungle
of loneliness,
so Lord, I pray,
for I can do no other.
I pray

to one who knows what it was
to be homeless,
moved on,
lonely,
hungry.
Lord, come with me,
walk with me
down these city streets,
and help me help these my brothers
and sisters
to know they are not alone,
but that we share and work and fight
and struggle together.
And that the 'we' includes you!

Amen.

# Freedom

Lord, can we talk?
Today, there was another massacre in South Africa.
People died,
    shot down.
They were unarmed,
    old,
    young,
    the bullets didn't care,
    but just tore into them;
    entering life one side,
    exiting death the other.


Innocent people,
    wanting to be free.
Free to live,
    when all that they're allowed
    is the freedom to die.
And they die, Lord.
They die!


And the world looks on,
    frowns with distaste,
    voices apparent disgust.
As it sits on the sideline.
A white sideline!
And the killing goes on.
Not just because they're black,
    but because they want to be free.

Freedom.
Is it really worth dying for?

Thousands believe it is,
    as from Soweto to South America
    they lay down their lives in its cause.

And what of us who are already free?
Do we care about the struggle?
Do we support those who fight?

Some do, with the weapons of
    sanctions,
    peace delegations,
    expulsion of ministers,
    Amnesty International,
    the UN.

Whilst somewhere,
    someone who is free
    uses that freedom to sell arms
    to both sides.

And the fight continues,
    as the concept of Freedom
    is shot to pieces,
    thrown into the blood of the innocent,
    and washed away by the tears
    of those who continue the fight.

Is it worth it, Lord?

All this death and destruction?

Can't you stop the killing?
Bring in freedom
    with the wisdom to handle it
    and the compassion to feed it?

Amen.

# I'll be on my way

Three people walking down the road,
   singing songs and hoping
   for future days to come.
Their footsteps mark those distant times,
   the good and the bad.
Drifting into memories
   as their lives move on.

The sun wanes over the horizon,
   warmth and light afresh.
Shine down life provider,
   and light up our way.
But the ghosts on the wind
   tell me, 'Don't stay'.
So again I realise I'll be
   on my way . . .

On I wander,
   over life's rocky shoreline.
The tide of pain ebbing
   over the sands of my mind.
As I follow again
   those footprints
   of the friend I have inside.

Three people walking down the road;
   their singing comes to an end.
As they face the crossroads,
   before them lies the choice decision.
   the narrow and the wide.

Voices beckon from ahead,
   as they ignore the one inside.

The moon rises slowly in darkness,
   its candle-like glow alive.
Shining down in sorrow
   as the three lose their way.
But the ghosts on the wind
   tell me to pray,
     that I may never, like the three,
     ignore the one inside . . .

Amen.